POSTCARD HISTORY SERIES

Grand Canyon National Park

Plateau Point, Grand Canon, Arizona.

Plateau Point is reached by way of a trail from the Indian Garden within the Grand Canyon. It offers a dizzying view to the Colorado River 1,000 feet below. (Courtesy of author's collection.)

ON THE FRONT COVER: The lengthening shadows of the late afternoon bring out the dramatic interplay of light and dark—chiaroscuro on a massive scale and a visual perspective measured in miles. (Courtesy of author's collection.)

ON THE BACK COVER: Built by the Santa Fe Railway and operated by the Fred Harvey Company, El Tovar Hotel, with its unparalleled view of the Grand Canyon, has greeted guests visiting the southwest for more than 100 years. (Courtesy of author's collection.)

POSTCARD HISTORY SERIES

Grand Canyon National Park

Thomas Alan Ratz

ARCADIA
PUBLISHING

Published by Arcadia Publishing
Charleston SC, Chicago IL, Portsmouth NH, San Francisco CA

Printed in the United States of America

Library of Congress Control Number: 2009931121

For all general information contact Arcadia Publishing at:
Telephone 843-853-2070
Fax 843-853-0044
E-mail sales@arcadiapublishing.com
For customer service and orders:
Toll-Free 1-888-313-2665

Visit us on the Internet at www.arcadiapublishing.com

To my parents:

For my father, Jerome Albert Ratz,
with his sense of humor and his storytelling.

In memory of my mother, Annabelle Marjorie Ratz,
for a life of love and support.

CONTENTS

ACKNOWLEDGMENTS

I would like to thank my editor at Arcadia Publishing, Jared Jackson, the southwest acquisitions editor, for being a wonderful guide on the writing of this, my first book. I also want to thank the personnel of the Grand Canyon National Park Museum Collection, Colleen Hyde, and the museum staff for their saintly patience with my odd inquiries, Michael Quinn for his encyclopedic memory, and Jan Balsom for guidance on the park service buildings.

I wish to thank my friends Paul and Kathleen Nickens for suggesting I do this book and Laura Jones for her much needed help with computer technology. I must also acknowledge my sisters and brothers for their familial support, Terry Pierce, Wendy Echtinaw, Theodore Ratz, Jill Kilsgaard, Todd Ratz, and Tammy Dankenbring.

Unless otherwise cited in this publication, all images have come from my personal collection.

INTRODUCTION

Greetings from the Grand Canyon.

This simple message is often written on picture postcards by vacationers to the Grand Canyon and mailed off to family and friends. However, there is some history to these ubiquitous mailings, particularly in relation to Grand Canyon National Park.

First off, postcards find their genesis in the private business mailing cards of 1861. In the United States, the picture postcard started when, authorized by an act of Congress in 1898, privately published postcards could be sent using standard rates, 1¢ in the United States and its island possessions, Cuba, Canada, and Mexico, and 2¢ elsewhere.

Since their creation, postcards have been an inexpensive method of sending messages home. They were also used as a note sent ahead to let the recipient know of the visitor's impending arrival. More often, the postcard was a low-cost souvenir of the vacationers' trip collected from all the places they had stopped to see. When finally home, the postcards were assembled in albums and brought out to show visiting family members. The postcard was also the perfect advertising tool. It would be purchased from the business shown on the card, and then the purchaser would pay to send this image out to a receptive, and perhaps future, client.

Secondly, the completion of several transcontinental railroads in the early 20th century made it possible for anyone with the money to travel across the country. Adventurer writers like George Wharton James and Charles F. Lummis came to the Grand Canyon, writing stories that appeared in Eastern newspapers. These stories created a romantic interest in seeing the Grand Canyon and the once Wild West. Seeing the business sense in advertising rail travel to the Grand Canyon on its trains, the Santa Fe Railway helped develop tourist facilities on the South Rim of the canyon. A longtime business partner of the railroad, the Fred Harvey Company, operated the hotels for the Santa Fe Railway. The Fred Harvey Company was completely responsible for the food service, overnight accommodations, and some of the publication of booklets, brochures, and postcards for the train traveler.

The Fred Harvey Company offered postcards for sale in the shops along the Santa Fe Railway. The images on the cards ranged from the tall buildings, fine homes, and parks of the cities the railroad passed through to rural scenes with celery fields, cotton-baling operations, and the scenic views of the passing landscape. Train travel across the United States could take several days. Travelers would write a short message on a postcard and drop it in a mailbox at one of the meal stops.

Postcards of the Grand Canyon were being produced by the late 1890s by several publishers and were sold in the first tourist hotels at the canyon. These hotels, the Grandview and the Bright Angel, each had post offices where visitors could send their correspondence home. With the arrival of the Santa Fe Railway at the Grand Canyon and the building of El Tovar Hotel in 1905, visitation greatly increased. The number of postcard images also grew.

The Fred Harvey Company had postcards published of its new hotel. Justly proud of El Tovar Hotel, the company had a great number of views produced of it, both of the exterior and the interior. The company also produced many postcards of other buildings at the Grand Canyon. The Hopi House, the Bright Angel Lodge, and the Lookout all had a series of postcards. The early images of these Mary Elizabeth Jane Colter designs are rich with the details of how the buildings first appeared.

Other businesses in the Grand Canyon Village also created postcards. The Kolb brothers made images of the canyon and the mule riders into postcards for sale in their studio. John G. Verkamp published a series of distinctive cards of the canyon that have a hand-colored look.

The Santa Fe Railway constructed more than structures at the Grand Canyon. It also built the Hermit Road as a means to avoid the tolls on the other canyon trails. Postcards were produced of the views all along this roadway and into the canyon along the trail to the river. Hermit's Rest was photographed from every angle, and these became picture postcards, too.

The Bright Angel Trail has long been the favored way to see the Grand Canyon from below the rim. Postcards of people riding mules and of the different sections of this trail were popular for tourists to send home, and many of these cards have short, handwritten descriptions of the rider's trip.

The establishment of the area as a national park in 1919 brought some order to the development that was taking place at the Grand Canyon. The building of better roads to the east of the village allowed visitors access to that part of the canyon. Services such as museums and interpretive displays where added to this part of the canyon to enhance the tourist experience. The building of the Watchtower in 1933 at the east entrance created one of the most iconic postcard images for the Grand Canyon.

The development of the North Rim of the canyon took longer because of its remoteness and the topography. The park service established the roads to the viewpoints on the North Rim and oversaw the tourist services built by the Union Pacific Railroad. The postcard images of the original and rebuilt Grand Canyon Lodge show the great effort the railroad put into its North Rim operation.

The great Colorado River has played an enormous part in the forming the Grand Canyon. The depth of the canyon has been determined by the erosion and cutting action of the river, but seen from the rim, the river looks small and belies the power it has. The river and its course were of great interest to the early explorers. Today the waters of the Colorado are used by white-water rafters on their memorable summer vacations.

Artists have had an important interaction with the Grand Canyon. Maj. John Wesley Powell invited landscape painter Thomas Moran along on his exploration of the Colorado River in 1873. Moran's paintings made visual the descriptions in Powell's report to Congress. The Santa Fe Railway hired many artists to produce Grand Canyon paintings for its advertising department. These romantic images of the West and the Grand Canyon, created for calendars and brochures, made a visit to the canyon a desire for the well heeled of the early 20th century.

The communities that are nearest the Grand Canyon but located outside the park boundaries were formed to aid travelers as they made their way to the national park. The businesses at these locations used postcards to advertise their services and their proximity to the park.

This book is arranged as a guide to the amazing number of postcards printed of the Grand Canyon. While not every card ever produced is shown here, this overview will give the reader an idea of how earlier tourists saw the Grand Canyon. The book is also laid out as a guide to the canyon itself. Each chapter covers a different aspect of the canyon that can be followed along the rim drives, some of the main trails into the canyon, or walking around the historic village.

One

HISTORIC GRAND CANYON VILLAGE

Visitors arriving at the Grand Canyon by train were greeted at this 1909 log station designed by Santa Fe Railway architect Francis Wilson. On the hill behind the station is El Tovar Hotel. Visitors could walk up the hill or a carriage would collect them for transport to the hotel. Note the tilde above the first *n* in Cañon. This was later changed to the Anglo spelling of Canyon.

H- 1387 HOTEL EL TOVAR AND THE HOPI HOUSE, GRAND CANYON, ARIZONA.

After arriving at the circular drive on El Tovar Hill, the visitor is flanked by El Tovar Hotel on the west and the Hopi House on the east. Just north is a low retaining wall, and just beyond, the Grand Canyon drops away. This is where most visitors had their first view of the Grand Canyon.

9900. HOTEL EL TOVAR, GRAND CANYON, ARIZONA. FRED HARVEY.

El Tovar Hotel is a fine example of the arts and crafts style of architecture. It uses Oregon pine and local stone. Architect Charles Whittlesey incorporated Norwegian villa and Swiss chalet motifs with a French mansard roof and rustic elements to create a building that is both distinctive and visually pleasing.

This view of the north wing of El Tovar Hotel shows the roof garden on the third floor with its obelisk-like posts. The second floor balcony reaches out to the canyon. The north porch offers a shady location to sit and watch people walk along the rim. The upper balconies used to be public areas but are now part of the north wing suites.

From the west looking east back at the hotel, this view shows the old water towers on the right, now removed. Water was brought by train cars from Del Rio, Arizona, just north of Prescott, a distance of 120 miles. The current water supply is from a spring inside the Grand Canyon.

79790 ENTRANCE TO HOTEL EL TOVAR, GRAND CANYON, ARIZONA

Sightseeing guests could depart from El Tovar Hotel via coach. The Fred Harvey Company built fine stables for more than 125 driving horses, saddle horses, and trail mules. There were also rooms for the coaches, wagons, saddles, and tack. This equipment was all first class, and the animals were well cared for.

12952 TRAIL PARTY IN FRONT OF EL TOVAR, GRAND CANYON, ARIZ. FRED HARVEY.

Guests taking saddle-horse rides along the rim or into the surrounding forest would find their mounts in front of the hotel. Because not everyone could pack for western adventures, and for the comfort of the riding guest, the hotel had a supply of divided skirts for ladies, gentlemen's overalls, linen dusters, hats, and more, which could be rented from the hotel for reasonable rates.

This view shows a large party leaving the hotel for a sightseeing tour. These usually were of short durations, two or three hours. Some could take the whole day, like the trip to Grandview, a 28-mile round-trip. There were even overnight trips that required guests to stay in tents. All the equipment and food were packed in the carriages that followed along.

As time passed, things changed, and the forms of conveyance changed, too. With automobiles, it was now possible to complete longer trips faster and to take trips farther afield. Now trips to Rainbow Bridge on the Utah border could be done from a Grand Canyon point of origin, and a trip to the Painted Desert was also possible.

Some greeting from your friend O. B. Reynolds (9/21/06)

When first entering El Tovar Hotel, visitors came upon the Rendezvous. A large room measuring 41 feet by 37 feet, the Rendezvous was noted for its walls of dark-stained logs and heavy rafters. Big game trophies repose above the plate rail that circles the entire room. Window seats offer a cozy spot for tête-à-têtes. Easy chairs and small desks allow one to read or write a postcard home.

A corner of the Office

A corner fireplace makes a charming sight on cold days. A newsstand is at hand for books and pamphlets of the Grand Canyon and for postcards to send to friends back home. The furniture was of the arts and crafts style and was made by the Stickley Brothers of Grand Rapids, Michigan. The style was used throughout the hotel.

The ladies lounging room was reached by the main stairs and was arranged around the octagonal rotunda. It was a place where the fair half of the world could sit without being seen, and chat, sew, or do any of a many inconsequential nothings to pleasantly pass the time. The walls of this space would have paintings and photographs of the southwest by artists like Thomas Moran or photographer Karl Moon.

Before the main dining hall, on the left, is a small private dining room. The wall decorations consist of intricate scrollwork wood panels. A plate rail with early china dishes circles this room. Above the plate rail is a Native American design of deer hieroglyphics reproduced from a prehistoric pictograph in Mallery's Grotto, a pictographic site at the top of the Bright Angel Trail.

According to an early Santa Fe Railway pamphlet, "When travel stains are washed off and fresh garments are donned, it is time for dinner. You enter a great Norwegian styled dining room eighty-nine by thirty-eight feet. Six huge log trusses support the roof. A dozen electric chandlers hang from these rafters. On the plate rail of the room rests old brass pots and antique Dutch and English platters."

There are matching fireplaces at each end of the dining room. This is one of the dining rooms where the famous Harvey Girls would serve fine meals prepared by capable chefs in a clean, modern kitchen. Daily deliveries by train kept this dining room supplied with seasonal foods. A local dairy brought milk and eggs to the kitchen. Greenhouses adjacent to the hotel supplied vegetables and flowers.

With time comes change. By the early 1960s, the arts and crafts–style dining room furniture was replaced. Large picture windows where installed. Murals painted by Hopi artist Bruce Timeche were placed around the dining room. These murals depict Native American ceremonies of the Hopi, Navaho, Apache, and Mohave. New chandlers in a quasi-prairie style replaced the rustic originals.

Changes came to the exterior, too. The shake-shingle roof was replaced with tar shingles. The packed-macadam drive was paved with asphalt. The arts and crafts–style furniture of the guest rooms was replaced with a rustic 1960s style. Of late, a shake-shingle roof has once again been added, and the hotel's furnishings have been replaced with a more stylistically pleasing form.

This postcard shows the view just north of the hotel. Here visitors are looking north–northeast. At the upper left is a short rock wall that serpentines along the edge of the canyon. This wall allowed visitors to stand at the edge and not have the anguish of getting too close to the precipice.

This 1906 postcard shows the view from close to the same spot as the one above but looking to the north–northwest. It gives a sense of how the canyon drops away without a slope in a near vertical cliff just beyond the retaining wall. Visitors would write home that this was the view from their hotel. Being this close to the Grand Canyon was the great enticement of El Tovar Hotel.

Visitors to the hotel were able to have their personal photographs developed in one day. The photographs could be printed on postcard paper stock. These images would be sent home to family members showing the travelers' progress on their great Western adventure. This 1920s postcard shows two ladies in their best flapper garb.

Employees at the Grand Canyon would also have their own real-photo postcards made. Here is a kitchen worker, posed with his pipe, waiting for the big rush of visitors to arrive. This 1915 postcard was sent to New York City. The message is written in French on the back. The Fred Harvey Company hired many first- and second-generation Europeans for positions at the hotel.

Just east of and adjacent to the hotel is the 1905 Hopi House. This irregular structure of stone was three stories tall, measuring 60 feet by 90 feet. It was the first building designed by Mary Colter and was built in the Grand Canyon Village. Only the National Park Service would have a greater effect on how buildings look at Grand Canyon than architect Mary Colter.

Mary Colter designed this picturesque building to resemble a Hopi pueblo block, complete with second- and third-story balconies and exterior staircases. Tall ladders for ascending to the upper floors lean against the walls. She did adjust traditional Hopi structural design by adding Anglo-style interior stairwells for the ease of the nonnative visitors.

Upon entering the Hopi House, one would have originally been greeted by a vast array of Native American art. The rugs on the floor were of Navaho manufacture, woven from the wool of sheep raised on the reservation lands. These amazing works of art are created by the Navaho women on an upright loom.

Also on display were native-made baskets. Nearly every Western American tribal group was represented, including the Hopi, of course, but also Apache, Havasupai, Navaho, Chemehuevi, Washo, Pima, Papago, Jicarilla, Walapai, Pomo, Maidu, Hupa, Yurok, Nootka, and Tlingit. All these colorful, intricately designed weavings showcased the amazing craftsmanship of America's native peoples.

Though Navaho rugs and blankets were scattered throughout the Hopi House, they were all for sale, usually for just a few dollars. This allowed Eastern visitors to take back a native-made work to remind them of their trip. Navaho rugs and blankets of this vintage now command high prices.

Also on display and for sale were pottery vessels by the Hopi, Zuni, and the pueblo people along the Rio Grande of New Mexico. These creations used native clays collected from the lands near the home villages, which were then fashioned into bowls and ollas and painted with mineral and vegetal pigments. As with basket weaving, pottery making was done mostly by women.

One room of the Hopi House was reserved for the arts of Pacific Northwest Native Americans. On display were totem poles, transformation masks, feast bowls, copper shields, and Chilkat blankets. The artistry of Native Americans from Washington State, British Columbia, and Alaska could also be purchased. This presentation gave the visitor a well-rounded overview of the exotic Native Americans.

The Fred Harvey Company's Indian Department became well known at the time for its diverse collection of Native American art and was so well respected that major American Indian art collectors and national institutions came to purchase from the Hopi House. The Smithsonian in Washington, D.C., the Natural History Museum in New York, and the Field Museum in Chicago all have items that were sold by the Fred Harvey Company.

Adding to the visitors' experience, the Fred Harvey Company had a kiva room. Through a low door, visitors would view altars similar to the ones created for Hopi ceremonies. This card shows the Tao altar. This altar is used while singing chants. Carved symbols of clouds, lighting, and cornstalks stand behind six ears of corn arranged around a medicine bowl. These altars were dismantled and removed a few years ago.

At the Hopi House there was a permanent display of old and rare pieces of Native American art. These items were not for sale but were meant to educate the public. In the 1960s, when the Fred Harvey Company was about to change ownership away from the descendants of the original founder, this Fred Harvey fine arts collection was donated to the Heard Museum in Phoenix, Arizona.

To add to the experience of a visit to the Hopi House, the Fred Harvey Company hired Native Americans to work and demonstrate craft making inside the rooms. This was much like the display presentations at world's fairs of the time, where whole villages would be on display. The Hopi House was a smaller, more intimate version of those exhibitions.

Here are several Native American demonstrators at the Hopi House. The man on the left is Hopi. He is making a wide sash used in ceremonial dances. The upright loom is traditional to the Hopi. Navaho weavers adopted this type of loom for their weaving. The woman on the right is Nampeyo. She was hired by the Fred Harvey Company to demonstrate pottery making. She was famous throughout her life for her amazing work.

This is another image of Native American demonstrators at the Hopi House. The Hopi woman on the left weaves a coiled basket of yucca and bear grass typical of the villages of Second Mesa. The man on the right weaves a Navaho blanket. This is an oddly staged postcard image. Navaho weaving is usually done by women, while Hopi weaving is done by men.

This image shows men singing around a drummer. This would be a scene in a real Hopi home or kiva, only there would be nether the Navaho rugs and blankets, nor the Pima baskets hanging from the ceiling. To the left of the men there are two pipes going up the wall. These are for the sprinkler system and the electric lights, both things not found a typical Hopi home of the day.

This view shows a group of Hopis on a roof terrace of the Hopi House. The woman standing on the left wears traditional garb—a dress of black, twilled wool with indigo diamond twill borders and a woven belt around her waist. Her hair is in the style of an unmarried woman. The young man on the right leans on one of the exterior staircases that lead to the upper terraces.

The Fred Harvey Company would hire entire native families to live and work at the Hopi House. This meant there were small children, too. The children were often dressed in complete miniature costumes that looked just like the adults. These children were a favorite subject for photographers.

27

H·3156   NAVAJO WEAVER, FAMILY AND HOGAN, GRAND CANYON NATIONAL PARK, ARIZONA

Demonstrations continued outside the Hopi House. There were Navaho hogans, the traditional Navaho dwelling, just to the east. Navaho men would fashion turquoise stones and hand-wrought silver into finely made jewelry. Navaho women would weave rugs from hand-carded and hand-spun wool. The hogans were replaced with the parking lot.

Native American dances were preformed to the north of the Hopi House. These performances had Hopi men and women dressed in their traditional clothing with added elements from other native traditions. This view shows an eagle dance with the drummer and singer wearing feathered headdresses not normally part of a Hopi performance. These types of dances are still performed and are popular.

Mrs. Amy Carpenter

ANYON SOUVENIR *Verkamp* INDIAN HANDICRAFT.

Here is a postcard showing Verkamp's curio shop. John G. Verkamp opened a store in 1906 selling Native American items and Grand Canyon souvenirs. This 1908 card shows the building with its flat roofs used to collect rainwater, which was cached in a cistern under the main floor. The family operated this business until 2008. This structure is now used by the Grand Canyon Association as a visitor's information center.

From El Tovar Hotel.

Verkamp's operated independently from the Fred Harvey Company and the Santa Fe Railway. The shop produced its own postcards and marketed them in the store. Verkamp's cards are easily spotted for their soft contrast and hand-colored look. The Verkamp family has had a long and important history at the Grand Canyon and in Arizona.

Log Cabin at Bright Angels, Grand Canyon, Arizona.
Photo SUB-POST Card Co., L. A.—Trade Mark.

East of El Tovar Hotel was the Bright Angel Hotel. This was the original hotel in the village. This complex consisted of a white clapboard main building with a registration desk and restaurant inside. Rows of tent cabins (a canvas roof and walls over a wood frame with a plank floor) were furnished with beds, linens, and a wood stove for heat in the winter. Martin Bugglen was the proprietor in 1903.

H-2768. BRIGHT ANGEL CAMP, GRAND CANYON NATIONAL PARK, ARIZONA.

Attached to the Bright Angel Hotel was Buckey O'Neill's 1880s log cabin. O'Neill was an early settler at the Grand Canyon. He worked mines in the area and was a local sheriff. He also served in Theodore Roosevelt's Rough Riders and died in the Cuba campaign. After El Tovar Hotel was built, the Fred Harvey Company took over this operation, and the Bright Angel Hotel became the Bright Angel Camp.

H-4470 BRIGHT ANGEL LODGE ON THE CANYON'S RIM, GRAND CANYON NATIONAL PARK, ARIZONA

In 1935, a new complex replaced the Bright Angel Camp. The Fred Harvey Company had a Mary Colter building put on this site. This stone, wood, and stucco group of buildings was designed to leave existing trees standing and to incorporate historic early structures like the Red Horse station and Buckey O'Neill's cabin. This new complex was named the Bright Angel Lodge and Cabins.

H-4478—NATIVE DEER ON STEPS OF BRIGHT ANGEL LODGE, GRAND CANYON NATIONAL PARK, ARIZONA

The Bright Angel Lodge has the design of a small village of buildings that naturally flow along the edge of the canyon. The front has a warm south-facing porch with benches. This is a nice spot to wait for the tour to start. Color was important to Mary Colter. She had a special shade of blue mixed as an accent color for this building's trim.

H-4472 THE LOBBY, BRIGHT ANGEL LODGE, GRAND CANYON NATIONAL PARK, ARIZONA

The open rustic lobby is warmed by high east windows and a great stone fireplace with inglenook seats on either side. Above the fireplace is a large wooden thunderbird. It has a Pacific Northwest Coast bird mask attached. This represents a spirit of the air—a bright angel.

H-4473 COFFEE SHOP, BRIGHT ANGEL LODGE, GRAND CANYON NATIONAL PARK, ARIZONA

The coffee shop is airy and lit with windows on the south and north sides. The north windows have glass transom panels painted with a combination of flower and organic designs. The ceiling is notable for the use of plaster vaults between the vigas. Much of this building has been remodeled during the intervening years, but it still retains its special character.

A cocktail lounge was added to the Bright Angel Lodge in 1958. This view shows the new lounge with its sleek mid-century style. Most important are the murals painted by famous Hopi artist Fred Kabotie. They show scenes of Hopi life, including farming, a plaza dance, and trading with Navaho neighbors. Architect Mary Colter knew artist Fred Kabotie; they collaborated on the decorations of an earlier building, the Watchtower.

This double-view card from around 1960 shows the exterior south entrance on top with few changes. The lower part of the card shows that the Western, rustic-styled furniture that Mary Colter originally put in the guest rooms was replaced with a simple efficient style typical of the time. Recently, the rooms have had makeovers, and a more appropriate arts and crafts style has been used.

On a rock promontory next to the Bright Angel Lodge, the Santa Fe Railway had another building designed by Mary Colter constructed. This 1914 structure was originally called the Lookout but is now known as the Lookout Studio. Colter's design is of uneven limestone walls that seem to be a part of the natural rock foundation with solid stairs leading down to terraces that have low walls along the cliff's edge.

H-1540. THE LOOKOUT, GRAND CANYON NATIONAL PARK, ARIZONA.

Some changes were made early on. Boardwalks lead tourists to the entrance. The profile of the chimney was made taller prior to 1921. Mostly, the Lookout stayed the same; even the small plants that Mary Colter had added continued to sprout from the top of the stone walls for many years. She wanted this structure to seem as if it had always been there.

A 1914 pamphlet by Santa Fe Railway reads, "Amid the quaint furnishings of the interior an ideal retreat was found. There surrounded by cozy seats was an open fireplace, sending its genial inviting glow throughout the rooms. Bright hued Navaho rugs, electric lights, and many Windsor backed easy chairs made for a pleasant place to contemplate the Grand Canyon or visit with a companion about the day's adventures." This card is postmarked December 1914.

The pamphlet continues, "A small library of books and pamphlets relating to the geology of the Grand Canyon were available. On the walls were maps showing the topographical nature of the region. On the tables were albums and portfolios with other images of the Canyon. Large windows offered views in all directions." This building is one of Mary Colter's small miracles.

H-1890 TELESCOPE AT THE LOOKOUT, GRAND CANYON NATIONAL PARK, ARIZONA

In the tower on the upper balcony was a large binocular telescope fashioned like an opera glass so anyone could, with minor adjustments, see 10 to 20 times greater than through a regular single-lens telescope. The North Rim of the canyon, though 13 miles away, appeared only half a mile distant through this device. Views of mule riders and trail hikers below the Lookout were also possible.

Anvil Rock, Grand Canyon.

Directly below the Lookout, jutting out from the canyon wall, is a sliver of stone in this card called the Anvil Rock. This looks dangerous; it must have been, because at one point the National Park Service erected a railing around the outer edge of it. The railing is no longer there, but there is no safe access to this point of rock today.

With the 1920s, many more visitors started arriving in their own private cars. An economical type of lodging was needed. The Fred Harvey Company built the Auto Camp Lodge. Visitors could check in, then drive their car to a nearby cabin. More rustic than the Bright Angel Lodge, the Auto Camp Lodge's accommodations gave the traveling family the option to stay in a room. This location has been replaced by the Maswik Lodge.

By the 1950s, even more accommodations were needed. In 1958, the Yavapai Lodge was built a mile to the east of the village. These single-story, motel-type units were designed by architect Roy E. Zollinger. The Fred Harvey Company had hired Lester B. Knight and Associate as the contractor. Additional units of two stories were added in the 1960s and 1970s.

This card shows the 1929 park service administration office building. Designed by architect Thomas C. Vint, this building, thanks to its natural architectural materials, blends harmoniously with the surrounding environment. This stylistic philosophy would continue to be used for many years throughout the national parks, with only the materials changing to suit the different locations.

At the end of World War II, with a great increase in visitation, there came the need to update park facilities. The governmental Mission 66 program placed many new visitors' centers in parks across the country. The visitors' center at the Grand Canyon, dedicated in 1957, is an example of the simpler modern style developed for park buildings. The visitors' center here was designed by Cecil Doty.

Two

THE HERMIT ROAD

A 1912 pamphlet described the new Hermit Road. "A most unique scenic roadway has been built by the Santa Fe from El Tovar westward to the head of Hermit Trail, a distance of about nine miles. It is called Hermit Rim Road. Engineering skill and a liberal purse have made possible a permanent macadamized thoroughfare that is wide, safe, and dustless and level as a floor."

The Hermit Road leaves the village and climbs Hermit Hill, earlier called El Tovar Hill. There are many opportunities to stop and view the canyon. The top-most stratum of the canyon is Kaibab limestone. There are many fossils found in this layer. These folks may be looking at fossils or just wanting a dramatic image. On average, about 12 people a year die in accidents in Grand Canyon.

7517 CAMPING PARTY IN TUSAYAN FOREST ON HERMIT RIM ROAD. GRAND CANYON, ARIZONA.

© FRED HARVEY

As part of a visit to the Grand Canyon, tourists could book camping trips with experienced guides through the transportation department. Fine meals were provided by the El Tovar Hotel kitchens and packed along. An overnight stay in a tent, surrounded by magnificent scenery in the fragrant pines, was often one of the trip's highlights for visitors.

This personally produced February 1912 postcard shows a well-to-do party in a carriage with El Tovar Hotel crests on the side enjoying an afternoon tour. Early visitors were usually of the well-off variety. Trips out west were expensive, time-consuming, and something of a novelty. A great number of the early visitors were the wives and daughters of the wealthy.

Once the top of Hermit Hill is reached, the road levels out. The views back to the village can give perspective to the scale of the canyon. El Tovar Hotel is just barely visible at the top and right of this card. The trail that is shown is the Bright Angel Trail.

This remarkable image shows the swimming pool that was at the Grand Canyon Inn. The inn was a lodging operation built upon the Lost Orphan Mine site. The mine was established near Maricopa Point in 1893 by Daniel Hogan. When the copper played out, he opened this lodge. In 1953, high-grade uranium was discovered. The inn was later closed, and this pool now only exists in a postcard.

Powell's Monument stands on what was Sentinel Point. It was dedicated on April 3, 1920, as a memorial to Maj. John Wesley Powell. This massive construction resembles an Aztec sacrificial altar and is made from native rock. This spot was also the location where the Grand Canyon was dedicated after the Congressional act of February 26, 1919, established it as a national park.

Just west of the Powell Memorial is Hopi Point. This is the highest and northern-most point along the Hermit Road. From here, visitors get more than a 180-degree vista. This card was produced and published by John G. Verkamp and gives the original name of this spot as Rowe Point.

East from (Hopi) Rowe Point.

This is another view from Rowe Point. Stanford Rowe, an early pioneer, operated a lodge south of this area. From his lodge, Rowe had a road to the rim that ended here. Names of the various points and rock formations have changed over time. The official names recognized by the park service are established by the U.S. Board on Geographic Names. Some postcards predate these established names.

From Rowe's Pt., Grand Canyon of Arizona.

H-4460   HOPI POINT ON THE GRAND CANYON RIM DRIVE, GRAND CANYON NATIONAL PARK, ARIZONA

Because of the spectacular view at Hopi Point, it is the favored destination for watching the setting sun. Most tours include this point as one of their stops. From this spot are visible some of the rock formations with fanciful names such as "the Alligator" below and "Cheop's Pyramid" across the river. These names were given to the rocky formations because of their resemblance to their title.

5043. GRAND CANYON OF ARIZONA, FROM ROWE'S POINT.
COPYRIGHT 1905, BY DETROIT PHOTOGRAPHIC CO.

The early reviewers of the Grand Canyon area always touted the clear year-round weather of the southwest. The views of the canyon change with the time of day and time of year. Atmospheric effects can change everything and some days completely obscure any view of the canyon. In winter, blinding snowstorms can make it very not-southwestern like.

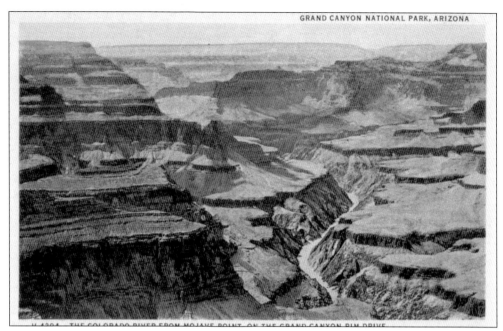

H-4304. THE COLORADO RIVER FROM MOJAVE POINT, ON THE GRAND CANYON RIM DRIVE

To the west is Mojave Point, where a good view of the Colorado River can be found. Just above the river is the Tonto Plateau, a wide flat section. This bench-like formation allows a natural route though the heart of the canyon. To the east is seen the Great Mojave Wall, a sheer cliff beneath Hopi Point. The sun can make this rock wall glow in the late afternoon.

5205. Sawtooth Mesa, Grand Canyon, Arizona.

As the sun sets, the shadows deepen the canyon silhouettes. Much is lost in the darkened shadows, but amazing details can be seen in the late afternoon light. The low angle of the sunlight makes the colors more pronounced; the reds and oranges become darker and the shadows more purple.

Looking down and northwest of Mohave Point, one can see Monument Creek. Erosion has left several pillars of brown sandstone. The greatest of them is called "the Monument," hence the name for the creek. It can be reached by way of the Tonto Trail between the Hermit and Bright Angel Trails.

Though the Hermit Road was well engineered early on, it was built for carriage traffic. Some improvements were needed for early automobiles and present-day car usage. Smoothing out sharp curves, widening the road bed, and easing the grades have made this road much safer and a beautiful ride.

This is a view of Cyclorama Point. Cycloramas were invented in the 18th century and became popular in the 19th century. They were large, cylindrical, panoramic paintings of historical events presented in circular rooms to give viewers the sense that they were seeing the events for themselves. Interestingly, a cyclorama was an artificial spectacle, while the Grand Canyon was a natural wonder.

Nomenclature is a changeable thing at the Grand Canyon. Cyclorama Point became Pima Point. Many names from the earlier times were changed. Now most of the points along the rim are named for Native American tribal groups. A few of these points are named for individuals with strong connections to the canyon's history.

The Arch at the Entrance, "The Rest House."   GRAND CANYON, Ariz.

At the end of the paved part of the road, there is a large stone arch with "HERMITS REST" in iron letters upon it. Atop the arch is an old school bell with a great crack in it. A lantern hangs from a rock projection, and a low wall stretches out from either side. This sight is the visitor's greeting at Hermit's Rest. Here is another creation of Mary Colter.

The Chimney, "The Rest House."
GRAND CANYON, Ariz.

Passing through the arch and ascending a small hill by way of large stone steps, a visitor will find a rock structure with a dome atop. This is the chimney. A step or two north, a visitor will find a viewing terrace with a sprawling vista of the canyon. At this vantage, the visitor will be atop Hermit Rest. This area is now closed to the public.

Hermit's Rest.   Grand Canyon, Ariz.

Continuing in the same direction past the chimney, another set of large stone steps will bring the visitor down to the west side of Hermit's Rest. This original way carried the walker over the top of the building. Mary Colter's design has the visitor interacting with the building rather than just walking to it. It can be entered by the west side porch.

The West Porch, Hermit's Rest.   Grand Canyon, Ariz.

Upon entering the porch, the visitor can see the roof section with the large, long log beams stretching out from the main part of the building. This roof is supported by wood posts and stacked stone pillars. The whole effect is of a building that was constructed by an old recluse living by himself at the end of the road. This is basically the "back story" of this building's design.

A large bear trap hangs on one of the support posts. Lanterns hang from the overhead beams. The original porch furniture was fashioned from branches and logs, allowing for places to sit and view the canyon in the shade. Tea and light refreshments were offered. Today's visitors enjoy ice cream and snacks under this same porch. Unfortunately, the original furniture is no longer.

The Entrance below, Hermit's Rest.
GRAND CANYON, Arizona.

On the east side of the porch, yet another set of large stone steps lead down from Hermit's Rest to a series of stone benches built into the hillside and a viewing terrace. Only fragments of this staircase remain because of washouts, and access to it has been blocked by a railing. Though this feature is lost, the building retains its charms.

The Fire-place, Hermit's Rest.   Grand Canyon, Ariz.

Entering the building, visitors are greeted by the feature it is best known for—a huge stone arch and great half-dome alcove with a fireplace set in the back. This is the hearth whose chimney was seen atop the entry hill. Architect Mary Colter had large fires built in this hearth so great black streaks of soot would darken the interior of the dome to make it look like it had been in use for centuries.

H-1343   VIEW, HERMIT REST, WINDOWS OVERLOOKING CANYON GRAND CANYON, ARIZONA.

Inside this main hall were scattered rustically made furnishings and a bear rug on a concrete floor that was patterned to resemble flagstone. A band of high clerestory windows offer light and ventilation. The front of the room has large windows looking out to the canyon. The thick support posts are painted with circular designs and have iron candelabra attached.

On the east side of the main hall, two arched doorways lead to the caretaker's room—a space with heavy ceiling rafters and wood-paneled walls. Another fireplace whose chimney forms a pinnacle outside offers warmth in this room. This would have been a cozy spot to chat and rest after the long carriage ride.

On the west side of the main hall, another pair of arched doorways led to the kitchen. When it first opened in 1914, Hermit's Rest had light refreshments for the visitors who ventured this far from the village. Tea and cakes were the norm. This kitchen still serves its original function, but it now serves sandwiches, ice cream, and snack foods.

Just west of the Hermit's Rest is the edge of the Hermit Basin, a side canyon off of the Grand Canyon. The Hermit Trail starts here and winds its way to the Colorado River. The other trails that break off from this one are the Waldron, the Dripping Springs, the Boucher, and the Tonto Trails.

In 1911–1912, the Santa Fe Railway built the Hermit Trail. It was constructed as a response to having to pay tolls on the Bright Angel Trail. Building this trail gave the Santa Fe Railway free access to the inner canyon. This access also gave another selling point to traveling by way of the Santa Fe to see the canyon.

Dripping Springs is a nice day hike down the Hermit Trail. Here is found the perennial spring that gives the trail its name. Louis D. Boucher, the hermit of the canyon, ran a tourist camp here in the early 20th century. He had tent cabins, fruit trees, and goldfish in a trough. He left the canyon area in 1912.

79812 BRIEF REST, HERMIT TRAIL, GRAND CANYON, ARIZONA

This trail was built on carefully surveyed engineering lines. It descends by easy grades on long switchbacks and zigzags though limestone and cross-bedded sandstone to the top of the red Supai layer. The westerly exposure of this trail allows for cooler starts in the morning and the protective shade of the high cliff walls.

H-2826 ON HERMIT TRAIL, GRAND CANYON NATIONAL PARK, ARIZONA.

The Hermit Trail was originally built as a private trail and was turned over to the park service in 1919, once the Grand Canyon became a national park. The park service now maintains the trail as funds become available. This trail has had several rock falls along it, but it is not too difficult to find the trail on the other side of the debris.

From the trailhead to the river is about 9 miles. Such a long trail would require several rest stops. Once the sun is high above, finding shade would be difficult. A rest house, built in 1913 at Santa Maria Spring, offers a nice respite. Vines grew over the rafters and made for a shady spot.

HERMIT TRAIL ABOVE SANTA MARIA SPRING, GRAND CANYON, ARIZONA.

Looking at the postcard images, one can see that many of them show mule riders on the Hermit Trail. This trail is no longer used as a mule trail. Once the Grand Canyon became a national park, the tolls on the Bright Angel Trail were lifted, and mule operations by the Fred Harvey Company were then concentrated on the Bright Angel Trail, a more convenient way to the village.

H-1542 ALONG THE CLIFFS ON HERMIT TRAIL, GRAND CANYON NATIONAL PARK, ARIZONA

H-2827 ON HERMIT TRAIL, 1700 FEET BELOW THE RIM, GRAND CANYON NATIONAL PARK, ARIZONA.

As the trail continues to the north, it clears the upper layers of the canyon, and the views open to the east. Early visitors called this spot Panorama Point. Not long after its abandonment, this section of the trail suffered rock falls and must now be negotiated by way of rock cairns.

5206. Great Terraces and River Gorge from Hermit Trail, Grand Canyon, Arizona.

A quick set of switchbacks brings the trail to Lookout Point. The terraces of the Tonto Plateau and the Inner Gorge are now in view. Looking to the North Rim, the buttes and great rock temples are now more pronounced against the sky and no longer blend in with background layers. Below here is the Hermit Creek Camp.

5201. Cathedral Stairs, Hermit Trail, Grand Canyon, Arizona.

The Hermit Trail reaches the edge of the Red Wall formation at the top of the Cathedral Stairs. This abrupt descent though the "blue" limestone reminded early writers of the twisting staircases of medieval churches. Here is the last of the great sets of switchbacks that bring the trail down to the Tonto Plateau.

The Hermit Creek Camp was built for tourists lodging overnight in the canyon. It was operated by the Fred Harvey Company from 1913 to 1931. At its height of operation, there was a dining hall, several tent cabins, a fruit orchard, and a vegetable garden. Water was supplied by the Hermit Creek, which ran just to the west.

The trail to the river followed Hermit Creek. A visitor would have descended along the trail in the shade of the Tonto Shale that had been cut away by the creek over thousands of years. The walls show layer upon layer of shale, and because it is fairly soft, the walls are nearly vertical. Flash flooding has deteriorated this trail.

After walking up Hermit Creek, there would be a plunge pool formed where the creek cascades over layers of shale and boulders. This pool is deep and large enough for a refreshing dip in the waters of Hermit Creek. Pools like this change their look over time because of the flash floods that frequent these narrow side canyons.

7510 BATH FALLS, HERMIT CREEK. GRAND CANYON, ARIZONA.

The trail to the river disappears into the alluvial rubble at the end of the Hermit Creek Wash. Picking a path to the river is not difficult. Once at the river, there is a view of the Hermit Rapids. Rapids form from the rock debris pushed into the river channel by flash floods coming down side canyons like Hermit Creek.

From Hermit Creek Camp, a return to the village was possible via the Tonto Trail. By heading east on the Tonto Trail, a connection to the Bright Angel Trail at the Indian Garden was made. This trail is relatively level, and it has no great elevation changes. The trail skirts around the side canyons of the Monument, Salt, and Horn Creeks. This trail transverses the canyon for more than 70 miles.

The views along the Tonto Trail are as spectacular as they are varied. The trail swings close to the edge of the Granite Gorge, with views of the Colorado River. It also passes beneath Pima, Mohave, Hopi, and Maricopa Points, which are more than 3,000 feet above, as it makes its way to the Bright Angel Trail and back to the village.

Three

BRIGHT ANGEL TRAIL

This February 1917–postmarked Fred Harvey Company postcard shows a group of tourists on mules about to descend into the Grand Canyon by way of the Bright Angel Trail. Minnie writes home to Philadelphia, "That they left at 9am. and returned at 5pm. That they were a jolly crowd and a tired looking bunch." This is the best sort of advertising.

Here are a couple of riders starting down the Bright Angel Trail packed for an extended camping trip. Prior to World War I, the best printed postcards were from Germany, as this card was. After the war, postcards for use in the United States became a domestic business. The Fred Harvey Company used the Detroit Photographic Company almost exclusively.

This advertising postcard is for the Kolb Brothers Studio. In 1903, Ellsworth and Emery Kolb set up a photographic business at the Grand Canyon. They took hundreds of photographs of mule riders astride their mounts. In the brothers' studio shop, they sold photographs of the canyon, hand-colored prints, stereo views, and postcards. Fiercely independent, Emery Kolb ran the business and lived at the canyon until 1976.

THE VIEW HUNTERS AT WORK IN THE CANYON.

This Fred Harvey Company postcard shows a group of riders posed at the start of the ride into the canyon. This is a sort of general image meant for visitors to write home about a mule ride they were just on. The Fred Harvey Company produced and sold a large number of images of the Bright Angel Trail.

This Kolb Brothers postcard demonstrates how the brothers were able to compete with the much larger Fred Harvey Company. They would produce personal postcards of the actual riders from a photograph taken at the start of the mule ride and have the finished card ready for purchase at the end of the trip. This image is from October 1916.

CAPE HORN, BRIGHT ANGEL TRAIL, GRAND CANYON, ARIZONA.

The Bright Angel Trail follows an ancient Anasazi pathway into the lower levels of the Grand Canyon. Pictographic sites are found along this route. To accommodate mule traffic, the trail is cut into and built on sheer cliff walls. This makes for dramatic images and harrowing stories by mule riders.

108—On "Cape Horn," Grand Canyon, Arizona.

This 1906 Kolb Brothers embossed postcard was sent to Chesaning, Michgan. The trail appears built of logs and rocks on the steep cliff side. The title "Cape Horn" refers to the dangerous nautical travail at the tip of South America, where many sailing ships lost their battle with the sea. Ship travel was still common at this date, and mule riders and hikers would have understood the reference.

As the Bright Angel Trail makes large switchback turns on its descent, it passes through groves of spruce trees. This species normally grows at a much higher elevation. The wall of the South Rim faces north, making it cool enough and wet enough for the trees to survive in these sheltering microclimates.

Views down Bright Angels Trail, Grand Canyon, Ariz.
Photo SUB-POST Card Co., L. A.—Trade Mark.

6326. GRAND CANYON OF ARIZONA, FROM JACOB'S LADDER.   COPYRIGHT, 1902, BY DETROIT PHOTOGRAPHIC CO.

Looking north from the trail, it becomes apparent that the vegetation changes dramatically. With the exception of where there is a creek or spring, plant life becomes typical of a desert region. Cactus of many types are found, along with cat's claw acacia, Mormon tea, prickly poppy, yucca, and Indian paint brush, and many of these plants have beautiful flowers that bloom in springtime.

This May 1915–postmarked Fred Harvey Company card shows a mule train on a section of the trail called Jacob's Ladder. This Biblical reference may be because there are so many switchbacks that angels could reach heaven on this trail. This card shows how the trail is cut into the cliff face.

The Bright Angel Trail was tied up in legal disputes in the early 1900s. Ralph Cameron, an early Grand Canyon settler and Arizona territorial senator, had mining claims on the length of this trail. This allowed him to charge tolls for the use of the trail. The Fred Harvey Company did not care for the tolls and built its own trail, the Hermit Trail. This conflict ended with the canyon's national park status.

The zigzags on the trails into the canyon are generally referred to as switchbacks. This economical way to descend steep elevations is common in the canyon. Proper manners has those going down the trail stepping aside for those going up, and everyone stepping to a safe location on the outside of the trail when mule trains go past.

79398 ZIG ZAG BRIGHT ANGEL TRAIL GRAND CANYON, ARIZONA

0325. ON THE ZIGZAGS, BRIGHT ANGEL TRAIL, GRAND CANYON OF ARIZONA.   COPYRIGHT, 1902, BY DETROIT PHOTOGRAPHIC CO.

Though the Bright Angel Trail was an ancient trail, it did have improvements made to it in the 1930s. Major changes to the top put the trail through two small tunnels. Several changes were done to make the switchbacks less steep, and the trail was widened. This may have lengthened the trail, but it is now easier on hikers, mules, and their riders.

Arriving at the Indian Garden, mule riders descend their mounts and rest a bit. This is the usual stop for lunch. Meals were packed down on the mules. There is also a campground here for hikers spending the night. A ranger station is staffed with park service personal. The block building was once part of a pumping station that sent water up to the village. The Tonto Trail connects here.

Here a John G. Verkamp postcard shows a group of mule riders milling about, waiting to remount for the remainder of their ride. Verkamp cards give the elevation changes. This one states that it is 3,180 feet below the rim. As the name infers, the Indian Garden was once a site for the Havasupai to grow crops and fruit trees. They were relocated to a camp on the rim, south of the village.

This personally produced real–photo postcard shows a family from Texas at the Indian Garden. The ladies wear high-necked buttoned-up blouses, long-sleeved jackets, and elaborate hats. Some of the men wear jackets and vests, and shirts with ties. This is not the norm today. The man on the white mule has a small child in front of him on the saddle. This card is postmarked November 1908.

Moonlight, Grand Canyon of Arizona.

Hiking the Grand Canyon at night has its own rewards. Many creatures that live in the canyon are active at night. Scorpions, bats, ringtail, and the Grand Canyon rattlesnake are usually found moving about in the dark. A full-moon night will also give great views of the canyon itself. It is even possible to make out the color of the cliffs with the light of a full moon.

From the Indian Garden, a trail goes out to Plateau Point. Great views into the Granite Gorge are possible here. This spot is 1,000 feet above the river, and there are views up and down the river. Across the gorge, the great rock formations now tower above, all but blocking the view of the North Rim. The South Rim stretches out behind.

7505. The Granite Gorge from the Plateau, Grand Canyon, Arizona.

Plateau Point is the turnaround spot for the day mule rides. After about a half hour at the point, riders remount. The mule train makes it way back to the Indian Garden and continues up Bright Angel Trail. The train makes several stops to look at the views during its return to the village.

From Indian Gardens, the Bright Angel Trail continues to the river. This card shows the group of switchbacks called the Devil's Corkscrew. This steep section of the trail is brutally hot in the summer months. In the early 20th century, this was a day trip. Mule trains were divided into those going to Plateau Point and those going to the river.

GRAND CANYON NATIONAL PARK, ARIZONA.

H.1508. THE DEVIL'S CORKSCREW ON BRIGHT ANGEL TRAIL.

During the Great Depression, the Civilian Conservation Corps (CCC) was established and assigned work in the Grand Canyon National Park. One of the CCC's great achievements was the building of the Colorado River Trail. This trail connects the Bright Angel Trail to the Kaibab Trail at the Kaibab suspension bridge. Work on this trail began in December 1933 and was finished in January 1937.

The building of the Colorado River Trail allowed visitors to follow the river for about 2 miles though the Granite Gorge. This is the only section of any major trail that has this feature. The Colorado River Trail gently rises and descends as it makes its way through the hard rock of the gorge. This rock is called the Vishnu Schist and is part of the earliest composition of the earth.

Looking Up the River from End of Trail—4500 Ft. Below Rim

This John G. Verkamp card shows an early view without the Colorado River Trail. The card states that it is 4,500 feet below the rim. The peak that is seen in the distance is called Zoroaster Temple. Its summit is more than 7,100 feet high. The river elevation is around 2,500 feet, making that peak nearly 1 mile higher.

This Fred Harvey Company postcard shows the first Kaibab suspension bridge. This structure was built across the Colorado River in 1921. It replaced a cable car system that was used as the main way to get to the north side of the river. Theodore Roosevelt would have used that cable car. This bridge was 420 feet long and 60 feet above the river.

The Kaibab Bridge made crossing the river much easier and allowed for more tourist visitation at the bottom the canyon. A wire screen was placed on each side of the bridge for the safety of the animals and people crossing on foot. The road bed of the bridge was made of wooden planks. All this material had to be transported by mule down from the South Rim.

Phantom Ranch, Grand Canyon, Arizona

On the north side of the river is the Bright Angel Creek. Following the creek up the north Kaibab Trail, one comes upon the Phantom Ranch. The CCC built a swimming pool here in the 1930s, one of their many projects at the Phantom Ranch and the Bright Angel Campground. This pool was damaged by a flash flood in the 1960s and was filled in.

H-4585   THE MAIN LODGE OF "DOWN-DEEP" PHANTOM RANCH

GRAND CANYON NATIONAL PARK, ARIZONA

The Phantom Ranch was developed by the Fred Harvey Company in 1922. The company had architect Mary Colter design a guest ranch consisting of a main lodge (pictured here), a group of guest cabins, and a recreation hall that was later used as the pool house and, when the pool was eliminated, was repurposed as employee housing. The large cottonwood trees were planted by the CCC.

This July 1929–postmarked card shows the Phantom Ranch complex lay out. The main lodge is in the center, the guest cabins are on each side, and a shower house is on the left. The development of the ranch took several years, since construction could not take place in the summer time. All materials except the rock had to be hauled down on mules.

This image, from above the Phantom Ranch, shows the view up Bright Angel Creek. The open area near the bottom was the location of the CCC camp. Visitors could write postcards and letters home from the ranch. A mail pouch hangs in the main lodge, where there is a rubber stamp for the correspondence to let the recipient know the item was taken out from the bottom of the canyon by mule.

The North Kaibab Trail continues up Bright Angel Creek to the North Rim for 14 miles. About 6 miles up the trail, a short side trail leads to the Ribbon Falls. Early on, this was called Altar Falls because of the large travertine formation at the base of the falls. This is a good place to wait out the heat of the day before continuing up the trail.

The North Kaibab Trail was greatly improved during the 1920s, replacing a more primitive trail that crossed the creek more than 90 times. Of the main corridor trails, this is the least crowded. The last 5 miles up are the steepest, and because the North Rim is higher in elevation than the South Rim, this makes for a more difficult climb.

Four

DESERT VIEW DRIVE

GRAND
CANYON
ARIZONA
and the
COLORADO
RIVER

as seen from

DESERT
VIEW

X6508

Though the Grand Canyon village is where most of the visitor facilities and the oldest building are today, some of the earliest tourist development took place to the east. Arizona Highway 64 connects the village with this historic and once-popular section of the canyon. This roadway is sometimes referred to as the East Rim Drive.

From El Tovar Hotel heading east on a smooth footpath, one comes upon Grandeur Point. As the name infers, the view is wonderful. This point also gives an overlook of the Bright Angel Trail, the Indian Garden, and Plateau Point. To the west is the Hermit Road.

H-3247. NORTHWEST FROM GRANDEUR POINT, GRAND CANYON NATIONAL PARK, ARIZONA.

Grandeur Point was the first viewpoint an early tourist would have stopped at on the carriage tour from El Tovar Hotel. This carriage ride was not long, about two hours round-trip, and it took in Yavapai Point also. This little ride gave a visitor several good views of the canyon in a short period of time.

Here a Detroit Photographic Company postcard, copyrighted in 1902, lists this view as O'Neill's Point. The point was named for Buckey O'Neill after his death on July 1, 1898, in Cuba during the Spanish American War. The point was later renamed Yavapai Point in keeping with the North American naming convention of the other viewpoints.

This artistic view card is from the Raphael Tuck and Sons publishers. The company was known for being appointed the art publishers to the king and queen of England. The cards would have a distinguishing blank space on the right side meant for a short message or greeting. This offset lithographic printing was done in Holland.

The Yavapai Point Observatory is 1.5 miles from El Tovar Hotel. This National Park Service building was constructed in 1929. Architect Herbert C. Maier used ponderosa pine and Kaibab limestone in a pueblo style to make an interesting structure that blends well with its surroundings. This museum has geologic displays and explains the layers of the canyon.

The views from Yavapai Point are excellent both to the west and east. From here, visitors are able to view parts of the river and see the Kaibab suspension bridge. The Phantom Ranch can be seen along the Bright Angel Creek through the cottonwood trees. To the east, the next point (Yaki) is visible, and the trail that descends from there can be made out in the layers of the canyon.

In 1925, the National Park Service completed the building of a trail from Yaki Point down to the river and at the spot the Kaibab suspension bridge crossed the Colorado River. This eliminated the need to pay a toll to ride down to Phantom Ranch. The top section of the trail has the nickname of "the Chimney" because of the steep set of switchbacks though the Kaibab limestone.

H-3988 TRAIL PARTY BELOW YAKI POINT ON KAIBAB TRAIL.
GRAND CANYON NATIONAL PARK, ARIZONA

This real-photo postcard shows a group of riders descending the "red and whites" set of switchbacks (the color of the trail changes from red to white on these switchbacks because the color of the rock formations changes on descent). Today trail rides do not descend the Kaibab Trail unless there are problems on the Bright Angel Trial. This trail is the shortest path to the river at 6.3 miles. The Kaibab Trail is well maintained and is part of the central corridor system for crossing the canyon.

The Kaibab Trail is aligned on a ridge into the canyon. This trail follows no creek bed, nor has it any springs on the way down, so there is no water available along the way. It is also exposed to the sun and has little shade. Plan to leave the rim early and take a large quantity of water, and this trail is a rewarding way to see the canyon.

With the new trail to the river, built in 1925, and increased visitation to the bottom of the canyon, the 1921 suspension bridge needed to be replaced. This new 1928 Kaibab suspension bridge is 440 feet long, 5 feet wide, and 65 feet above the river. The new bridge allowed more traffic to move over the Colorado River at one time.

Continuing eastward on Desert View Drive, 6 miles from El Tovar Hotel, a turnout offers distant views to the north and east. The rock layer at the uppermost level of the rim has eroded into a fantastical form called Duck on the Rock. A bit of imagination is needed to recognize the duck.

6324. THOR'S HAMMER, GRAND CANYON OF ARIZONA.

Farther along the drive, other turnouts have more of the fanciful rock forms with imaginative names. This rock pillar is called Thor's Hammer. A modern audience might not know the reference, but this stone "hammer" is large enough for the great Norse god to use it to kill giants. There are many versions of this postcard, and they were issued for many years.

83

Prior to El Tovar Hotel being built in the Grand Canyon village, the Grand View area of the canyon saw more tourist development in the late 19th and early 20th centuries. Building upon his mining claims that were slowly playing out, Pete Berry finished construction on his log hotel in 1897. He called this new enterprise the Grand View Hotel.

In 1902, Pete Berry sold his mining claim that the log hotel sat on to a mining interest operated by Harry Smith, who had extensive mines below the rim of the canyon. In 1903, Berry built a three-story hotel on his homestead that was next to his old mining claim, calling it the Summit Hotel. Berry and Smith then operated these ventures jointly as the Grand View Hotel.

This personally made June 1906 postcard has the handwritten note, "Out with the ranger for a 30 mile ride thru the beautiful Coconino forest." Thirty miles is roughly the round-trip mileage from Grand View to the Grand Canyon village. The ranger would be a forest ranger. The forest service administered the Grand Canyon at this time, since the National Park Service had yet to be created.

Although the Grand View Hotel was isolated, it did offer amenities similar to Eastern hotels. After travelers' two-day stage ride, they would find a hotel with steam heat, warm baths, fresh spring water, and hearty meals prepared by Martha Berry. The hotel had a small library and a post office, so an extended stay was possible, and the visitor would not feel cut off from the outside world.

THREE CASTLES.   VISHNU TEMPLE.   PAINTED DESERT.
                                                              MORAN'S POINT.

GRAND CANYON OF ARIZONA FROM NEAR GRAND VIEW   COPR. DETROIT PUBLISHING CO.

Another amenity the early visitor to the Grand View Hotel would find was the overlooks of the Grand Canyon in this area, which are, in many ways, much nicer than the views from El Tovar Hotel. There were riding trails along the rim to the east that had views of the Painted Desert and the eastern edge of the canyon.

FROM THE OUTLOOK, GRAND VIEW, GRAND CANYON, ARIZONA.

The competition from El Tovar Hotel, with its rail access and powerful backing of the Santa Fe Railway, was too strong. The Grand View Hotel closed in 1907. Eventually, Pete Berry sold these hotel properties to William Randolph Hearst. The older hotel was dismantled in 1929. The logs were salvaged and were used in a Mary Colter–designed building at Navaho Point—the Watchtower.

86

5473. THE GRAND CANYON OF ARIZONA.
COPYRIGHT, 1900, BY DETROIT PHOTOGRAPHIC CO. *Feb. 1903.* *J. W. L.*

The Grand Canyon is most noted as a scenic wonder, but this was not the only aspect early settlers saw. With such a large area of exposed land, mining was one of the first uses for the Grand Canyon. Many old mines can be found throughout the canyon area. The Grand View section had many mines extracting mostly copper, with minor amounts of gold and silver.

In pursuit of any ore that could be found in the Grand Canyon, the miners had to build trails into the areas that had the best chance of producing. The ore that was extracted from mines inside the canyon was than hauled out on burros. The ore would be taken by wagon to a railhead and shipped to a mill as far away as El Paso, Texas.

6326. STARTING DOWN GRAND VIEW TRAIL, GRAND CANYON OF ARIZONA.
COPYRIGHT, 1902, BY DETROIT PHOTOGRAPHIC CO.

The trail into the canyon off Grand View Point was originally a mining trail. It is steep and winding. It is also cleverly built, with large sections of log cribbing and rock cobbles. The trail that descends from Grand View was redesigned as a tourist trail in 1902 for the use of mule riders and those hiking into the canyon.

With the building of the trail down from Grand View, the miners of the Grand Canyon became trail guides. Three miles down this trail is Horseshoe Mesa. This relatively flat area was the location of much of the mining operations. Mining took place even while tourists visited. Some remnants of the early mining times are still visible off the east side of the mesa.

Caves were discovered on the western side of Horseshoe Mesa in 1897 by the copper mines' cook, Joseph Gilder. This cave system became popular with the early tourists. George Wharton James wrote in 1910 that "stalactites and stalagmites were numerous and diverse, that sheets of calcareous deposits hung like curtains." Nearly all these decorations are gone from souvenir hunters snapping them off and taking them away.

Granite Gorge from Grand View Plateau, Grand Canyon, Arizona.

From Horseshoe Mesa it was possible (and still is) to descend to the Tonto Plateau level. This can be done on the east and west sides of the mesa. These trails connect with other inner canyon trails. One trail leads to the edge of the Tonto level with a long view of the Colorado River. Descending to the river from here is difficult.

The original road from Grand View did not follow the edge of the canyon. The road continued east-southeast though the Coconino forest, skirting the Little Colorado River Gorge to the Cameron Trading Post. A spur road would take visitors to the overlook known as Desert View. This Raphael Tuck and Sons card labels this as Bissell's Point when in fact it is Moran Point.

H-4214   THE INDIAN RUINS AT MORAN POINT, GRAND CANYON NATIONAL PARK, ARIZONA

In the early 1930s, the National Park Service reoriented the road closer to the canyon's edge, making the road more scenic and giving easier access to the viewpoints along the rim. This Fred Harvey Company card shows the east side of Moran Point, named for the great British-born American landscape painter Thomas Moran. This is one of the rare points not named for Native Americans.

Between Grand View and Moran Points is one of the historic trails into the canyon. The Hance Trail was built in the early 1880s by John Hance to access his mining claims. By 1886, "Capt." John Hance found being a guide to Eastern visitors a better profession then a miner. His camp accommodations may have been rustic at best, but his storytelling knew no equal.

5474. HANCE'S TRAIL, GRAND CANYON OF ARIZONA.

7428 WALLS OF THE GRAND CANYON, FROM BISSEL'S POINT

An 1899 Detroit Photographic Company postcard lists this view as Bissel's Point, named for a Santa Fe Railway executive, as several in this area were. This point was renamed Zuni Point, in keeping with the Native American names of the rim points. The U.S. Board on Geographic Names now oversees the names used on official maps, and it is more difficult to change or assign new names.

H-4215 WAYSIDE MUSEUM OF ARCHAEOLOGY, GRAND CANYON NATIONAL PARK, ARIZONA

The Grand Canyon has a long and ancient history of human habitation. The small Tusayan Museum along the East Rim Drive has displays of the 4,000-year-old split twig figures found in caves below the rim of the canyon. Prehistoric pottery and other materials excavated from a nearby ruin are also on view. An interpretive trail around the ruin explains the living conditions of these early farmers.

7521. Morning after a Storm, Grand Canyon, Arizona.

Rains during the summer monsoons and the winter snowpack allowed these ancestral pueblo people to grow crops such as corn, beans, and squash. Evidence of ancient farming is found in the washes on both sides of the canyon and along the creek beds inside the canyon near the river. Planting small fields in different locations helped ensure there would be enough food for all the inhabitants.

The ancestral farmers of the Grand Canyon would store some of their harvest of corn in granaries built below the rim of the canyon. The granaries were made of stone and mud sealed from the weather and rodents. These were built into the walls of the canyon on near-inaccessible ledges. Some of these granaries have been found still intact beneath the rim.

H-3989   LOOKING NORTH FROM DESERT VIEW ROAD

H-3248. AN EARLY MORNING VIEW FROM LIPAN POINT, GRAND CANYON NATIONAL PARK, ARIZONA

These ancient people of the Grand Canyon are gone, but they left behind nearly 4,800 archaeological sites in the area. There are sites on the South Rim inside the canyon and on the North Rim. Most of these sites have not been excavated or cataloged. These sites, when found, should be left undisturbed for future visitors to enjoy.

By 1932, the road alignments of the Desert View Drive brought the road to the eastern edge of the park boundaries. With these improvements, views of the Painted Desert and the confluence of the Little Colorado River were easily accessible. These roads also helped established the park service's dominance in any new development that would take place.

All new development in the Grand Canyon National Park was now solely at the discretion of the park service. Future building of any facilities would need federal approval and would happen when and where the park officials saw the need. Services and accommodations for visitors became the focus, and mining of ore became part of the Grand Canyon's history.

In the early 1930s, the park service saw the need for visitors' facilities in the Desert View area. The National Park Service engaged the Fred Harvey Company for this new development. The Fred Harvey Company had architect Mary Colter design a new building for this location. Her concept was a tower similar to ones she had seen at the Hovenweep National Monument, the Mesa Verde National Park, and the Canyon De Chelly National Monument.

H-4219   THE WATCHTOWER AT DESERT VIEW, GRAND CANYON NATIONAL PARK, ARIZONA

Mary Colter's Watchtower at Desert View is much grander then any of its prehistoric antecedents. Thirty feet across at the base and 70 feet tall, at four stories it is also her tallest structure. This ancient-looking building with its stone walls reaching a great height actually has a steel superstructure designed by Santa Fe bridge architects and concrete footings.

The Desert View Watchtower was dedicated on May 13, 1933. The dedication included a group of Hopi men blessing the tower and the adjoining kiva room. This dedication ceremony was covered by national newspapers, radio, and even newsreel motion pictures shown in theaters across the country. The exterior of the tower has the occasional stone protrusion, causing shadows to play along its surface. There are slabs of stone with petroglyphs incorporated into the interior and exterior. A large viewing terrace is atop the kiva section of the building. This beautifully composed postcard shows people atop the tower, but the public is not allowed on that level today.

Upon entering, the first room is the kiva. This large circular space is based on the great kivas like the ones at the Aztec National Monument and the Chaco Canyon National Historic Park. The Hopi build rectangular kivas. The ladder represents the traditional method of entering a kiva. At the base of the ladder is the fire pit. The smoke from the fire would exit the opening the ladder ascends to.

The ceiling of cribbed logs was salvaged from the old Grand View Hotel. Scattered around the room is rustic furniture made from tree trunk and burls covered with rawhide. The large picture windows frame views of the canyon and the desert to the east. Reflectoscopes of black glass, attached to the side of the windows, allow viewers to see small portions of the canyon with more intense color.

On the first floor of the tower is a re-creation of a snake ceremony altar. Crooked wands flank a sand painting of four snakes surrounding a mountain lion. Standing behind the sand painting is a representation of one of the snake priests. Arranged on the perimeter are lighting frames, feathers, pouches to hold snakes, and a large canteen to wash the snakes—all objects to aid in bringing rain.

The main mural on the wall of this room is by Hopi artist Fred Kabotie. It depicts the story of a man who navigates the Colorado River and discovers the snake people. Other figures from Hopi mythology are on adjoining walls. On the walls of the upper levels of the tower are recreations of cave art, petroglyphs, and pictographs from the surrounding area.

Five

THE NORTH RIM

A134. Grand Canyon Lodge, North Rim Grand Canyon of the Colorado

The North Rim of the Grand Canyon is, in some ways, the distant shore of the park. It is remote, with no direct rail line, and its harsh winters shorten the visiting season. With its higher elevation and difficult topography, the north side of the canyon is very different than the South Rim. Large-scale development did not arrive there until the late 1920s.

The greatest example of development on the North Rim was the completion in 1928 of the $550,000 Grand Canyon Lodge at Bright Angel Point. Built by the Utah Parks Company from a design by Union Pacific Railroad architect Gilbert Stanley Underwood, it became the center of the tourist activity at the North Rim. This large building complex of limestone and ponderosa pine blended well with its surroundings.

Grand Canyon Lodge, North Rim, Kaibab Forest, Arizona

Tragedy struck on September 1, 1932. A devastating fire destroyed the main building. The Utah Parks Company rebuilt the lodge in 1936–1937 at the same location with a slightly reduced silhouette. The new lodge was constructed with more exterior stonework in place of the timber, and the lodge changed from the Californian craftsman type to a simpler rustic style.

A138. Grand Canyon from Terrace of Grand Canyon Lodge. On the North Rim.

The Grand Canyon Lodge has large terraces on the south side of the building. These make a sunny place to relax. From here, the canyon drops away with the great temples in plain view. The South Rim is visible, and in the far distance, the San Francisco Peaks near Flagstaff can be seen. An oversized fireplace on the terrace was the meeting place for the evening ranger talks.

Sun Lounge, Grand Canyon Lodge, North Rim, Grand Canyon National Park

On days when the weather is too cold for sitting outside, there is the spacious observation lounge—a place to watch the cloud shadows play on the buttes and temples of the canyon. The furniture is a collection of rattan sofas and chairs. There are small writing desks available. Navaho-styled rugs on the floor and large Native American–designed chandlers light this room in the evening.

Inside the main lobby of the Grand Canyon Lodge is the registration desk for the guest cabins. On the east side of the lobby is a recreational hall, to the north is the observation lounge, and on the west side is the dining room. Upon entering the dining room, guests are escorted down a flight of steps to their table. An organist, on the left in the image, provides music for the diners.

Dining Room, Grand Canyon Lodge, North Rim, Grand Canyon National Park

The dining room has large wood trusses at the ceiling with a steep pitch to shed the winter snow, and four chandeliers for after-sunset dining. Huge windows look out onto the Grand Canyon. Waitresses at the lodge were often college students, since this was a summertime operation. After dinner, the staff would provide musical entertainment in the recreational hall.

On the east side of the lodge are the deluxe cabins. Two cabins were lost in the 1932 fire. These cabins offered the elegance that the wealthy traveler of the time expected. The deluxe cabins show the original style of the Gilbert Stanley Underwood architecture. Other, standard cabins on the west side of the main lodge have a more rustic look and were for the more modest budget.

The Utah Parks Company also operated the Grand Canyon Inn, built in 1929 by the Union Pacific Railroad. This small facility, around a mile from the main lodge, rented small, economic tourist cabins. Its restaurant catered to the cabin tourists and those staying in the nearby campground. This operation is still open but is now a general store and supply location for hikers.

A119. Bright Angel Point, from North Rim, Grand Canyon National Park

The viewpoints on the North Rim give a very different perspective of the canyon. The large buttes and temples in the Grand Canyon that on the South Rim are seen at a great distance are much nearer on the North Rim. This postcard is of Bright Angel Point, a short hike from the Grand Canyon Lodge, which gives an overlook of the north Kaibab Trail.

THE GRAND CANYON from Panorama Point.

This is a Raphael Tuck and Sons card from around 1907 of Panorama Point. Interestingly, early maps have no listing for a "Panorama Point." This image was placed in this section because the general view shown looks to be the north side of the canyon. This British postcard publisher lost all records of the earlier images when its factory burned during a bombing raid in 1940.

104

The Union Pacific Railroad's nearest train station to the Grand Canyon was in Cedar City, Utah, 187 miles northwest. Visitors traveling to the North Rim would book tours with the railroad and were taken by motor bus. A minimum three-day booking was needed to do the round-trip. Guests would stay at the Grand Canyon Lodge, visiting other national parks on the way there and back.

ANGELS WINDOW, NORTH RIM, GRAND CANYON, ARIZONA

At the end of Cape Royal is a large natural formation called Angels Window. Erosion has pierced a thin spur of limestone that juts out into the canyon. A railing around the top of the formation allows for dizzying views across the canyon. This amazing point is one of the most iconic images of the Grand Canyon on the North Rim.

VISHNU TEMPLE FROM CAPE ROYAL, NORTH RIM OF THE GRAND CANYON

The park service improved the roadways to the viewpoints on the North Rim. Roads to Point Imperial and Cape Royal were completed in 1927. With the new roads and the 1928 opening of the lodge, the Union Pacific Railroad had as fine a Grand Canyon operation as that of the Santa Fe Railway on the South Rim, and it also used images of the Grand Canyon on many of its advertisements and brochures.

There is roughly a 1,000-foot elevation change on the North Rim. The vegetation there is different than that on the South Rim. The high forests of the North Rim have spruce, hemlock, aspens, and other mountain species. Large open meadows, called parks, with prairie grasses, support herds of deer, which are often seen while entering and exiting the park.

Six

THE COLORADO RIVER

THE GRAND CANYON.
Colorado River
in Glen Canyon.

With its source in the central Rocky Mountains, the Colorado River builds in volume and strength with the additions of the Gunnison, Dolores, Green, and San Juan Rivers. The Colorado River has carved Glen Canyon and Marble Canyon. This great river then cuts through the layers of the Colorado Plateau, creating the Grand Canyon. The Colorado River drains 242,900 square miles by the time it reaches Mexico.

The Colorado River is more than 1,450 miles long, with 227 miles through the Grand Canyon. The Glen Canyon dam, built in 1962, changed the water flow through the canyon dramatically. Explorers of an earlier day faced the rapids of the Grand Canyon with no special knowledge of the stretches of smooth but swift water in between spectacular rapids.

In 1858, explorer Lt. Joseph Christmas Ives was assigned the task of determining the navigability of the Colorado River for the U.S. War Department. This great endeavor ended poorly. Ives became discouraged and wrote that this was a "profitless locality" and "shall be forever unvisited and undisturbed." Maj. John Wesley Powell was the first to systematically survey the Colorado River in 1869 and again in 1872.

In 1889, Frank M. Brown and Robert B. Stanton led a survey party to determine if a railroad could be built along the Colorado River. This trip suffered the drowning of three of its members, including Brown. The plan for a rail line along the river never came to be. Visitors to the Grand Canyon rarely see more than a glimpse of the river from the rim viewpoints.

Prospectors would use the river as a way to search for possible mining claims. Announcements of large veins of gold and silver found in the Grand Canyon would show up in the newspapers at the beginning of the 20th century. None were found. Some of these early pioneers would access the river for fishing.

This 1912-postmarked Fred Harvey Company card has on the back a long description of Charles Russell and E. R. Monett running the Sockdologer Rapid. Russell and Monett were prospectors searching for gold in the Grand Canyon. Their arrival at Needles, California, in February 1908 was covered in the national papers. The story had many of the details of their dangerous journey. *Sockdologer* means exceptional, or final blow.

A July 21, 1947–postmarked card shows Norman Nevills shooting one of the many rapids in the Grand Canyon. This expedition was the subject of the *National Geographic* August 1947 issue. Nevills created the idea of commercial white-water rafting in 1938. He ran his rafting business out of Mexican Hat, Utah, until he and his wife, Doris, died in the crash of their small airplane in 1949.

This real-photo postcard is from a photograph by the Kolb brothers. The remarkable image shows the view at the river level, and the rim of the canyon can be seen in the far distance. Their use of light and shadow is apparent here. The Kolb brothers did a river trip in 1911 starting at Green River, Wyoming. They navigated the Green River to its confluence with the Colorado River, down through Utah and the Grand Canyon. Eventually, they ran the river all the way to the Gulf of California. They photographed and filmed this trip. This silent motion picture was presented daily in the auditorium of their studio on the rim with Emery Kolb doing the narration.

79079 A QUIET STRETCH NEAR END OF GRANITE, GRAND CANYON, ARIZ.

The National Park Service regulates the number of people that raft the Colorado River through the Grand Canyon. There are commercial companies contracted with the park service. Private trips are allowed and are assigned by an allotment system. Today around 22,000 people raft the Colorado River through the Grand Canyon each year.

EMERY FALLS, UPPER END OF MEAD LAKE IN GRAND CANYON

The Colorado River through the Grand Canyon is bookended by the Glen Canyon dam above and Lake Mead below. The river finishes it run through the Grand Canyon when it reaches Lake Mead. Pleasure boaters can travel a short way up the Colorado by way of Lake Mead. One of the sights that can be seen this way is Emery Falls (also known as Columbine Falls).

Seven

GRAND CANYON ARTISTS

In 1873, Maj. John Wesley Powell invited the British-born artist Thomas Moran on his survey of the Grand Canyon. Moran's oil paintings and watercolors of the canyon became the first images of the canyon that Easterners saw. His 84 3/8-by-144 3/4-inch painting *Chasm of the Colorado* hung in the national capitol. The Santa Fe Railway used Moran's pictures and images of him sketching in its advertisements.

The Santa Fe Railway hired many artists to create paintings for its brochures and advertisements. In 1905, the railroad had Louis Akin (1868–1913) paint the new El Tovar Hotel. This painting was reproduced many times, and chromolithographs of this image were placed in railroad stations along the Santa Fe Railway line. This is a 1907-postmarked card.

The earliest produced postcards were often artist's renditions of historical scenes or domestic life. The tradition of using artists continued well into the 20th century. The benefit of artist images over photography was the use of color and the ability of the artist to create the perfect image. Gunnar Widforss (1879–1934) was a master of the watercolor medium and one of the best chroniclers of the Grand Canyon.

Over time, many artists worked for the Santa Fe Railway, producing paintings for the railroad's advertising department. The Zoroaster Temple was a popular subject. This painting by Norwegian-born Chris Jorgensen (1869–1935) is similar to views on page 72. Here the artist is able to compact the composition into a strong vertical to create a sense of great height. This painting hangs in the dining room of El Tovar Hotel.

H-1523   THE GRAND CANYON, ARIZONA

79005   GRAND CANYON, ARIZONA.   COPR. FRED HARVEY

This view of Zoroaster Temple is by British-born Edward Frederick Ertz (1862–1954). He had a career as an engraver and later studied in France. His work was shown at the Columbian Exhibition in 1893, at the St. Louis Exhibition in 1904, and at the Panama-Pacific Exhibition in 1915. Ertz became a professor of watercolor at the Delecluse Academy in Paris, and he was a member of the Royal Academy of Artists in England.

At the suggestion of Stephen Mather, Gunnar Widforss traveled to many national parks to paint, but he always returned to the Grand Canyon. When at the canyon, Widforss would stay with the Kolb family. He also had an arrangement with the Fred Harvey Company. He lived in the company's dormitory and received meals. In exchange, he produced artwork that was sold in the art rooms of El Tovar Hotel.

"THE FIREPLACE"—HERMIT'S REST, GRAND CANYON NATIONAL PARK, ARIZONA.   FROM PAINTING BY GUNNAR WIDFORSS.

The Fireplace, by Gunnar Widforss, is the interior of Hermit's Rest. Widforss painted many subjects in and around the canyon, including scenes at the river and at the Phantom Ranch and of the forest in summertime and in the winter. He had a great ability to capture the light of a particular time of day on geological features.

This imaginative postcard of a painting by Harold Harrington Betts (1881–1951) has mule riders stopping on the trail to view the Grand Canyon with a Native American. Betts was born in New York City into a prominent artist family. He traveled west in 1913 and 1929 and was known for his Grand Canyon scenes and Native American images.

Titian of Chasms, by William Robinson Leigh (1866–1955), was commissioned by William Simpson of the Santa Fe Railway. This painting was used for the cover art of the large brochure advertising the canyon, on the cover of menus for the railroad's dining cars, and, of course, on postcards. Leigh had a long, distinguished career. His draftsmanship and attention to detail earned him the title of the "Sagebrush Rembrandt."

"THE WATCHTOWER AND THE COLORADO RIVER"—DESERT VIEW, GRAND CANYON NATIONAL PARK, ARIZONA. FROM PAINTING BY GUNNAR WIDFORSS.

After the Watchtower was completed in 1932, the Fred Harvey Company asked Gunnar Widforss to do a series of watercolors of the building. These images were made into postcards and packaged with other Widforss images as a group in an envelope. The group was sold in all the retail shops in the Grand Canyon and in shops along the Santa Fe rail line.

"THE KIVA"—DESERT VIEW, GRAND CANYON NATIONAL PARK, ARIZONA. FROM PAINTING BY GUNNAR WIDFORSS.

Widforss painted both exterior and interior views of the Watchtower. This interior, *The Kiva*, adds the imaginative embers and smoke in the fire pit, but no fire was ever built there. The five windows allowed for five canyon studies, with the shadow-heavy west window on the left and a bright, sunlit view on the right.

A rocky spur juts out from the rim below the Watchtower. A short hike down to this point gave Widforss the low angle to paint this *Worm's Eye View*. This painting shows how the tower appears to grow right up from the rim of the canyon and the tower's unique profile outlined against the sky.

"THE WATCHTOWER"—DESERT VIEW, GRAND CANYON NATIONAL PARK, ARIZONA.

"VISTA THROUGH KIVA WINDOW"—DESERT VIEW, GRAND CANYON NATIONAL PARK, ARIZONA.   FROM PAINTING BY GUNNAR WIDFORSS.

In *Vista Through Kiva Window*, Widforss created a frame–within–a–frame view of the canyon and the river. This also highlights the kiva windows as true picture windows. The windows allowed a viewer the ability to contemplate the canyon in small sections and study the view without having to try to take in the whole canyon at once.

"SUNSET ON THE PAINTED DESERT"—FROM THE WATCHTOWER, GRAND CANYON NATIONAL PARK, ARIZONA.   FROM PAINTING BY GUNNAR WIDFORSS.

In 1924, seventy-two of Gunnar Widforss's watercolors were exhibited at the National Gallery of Art in Washington, D.C. In 1925, the president of the Yosemite Park and Curry Company made a similar arrangement with Widforss as at Grand Canyon. Widforss would produce paintings at a reduced cost in exchange for room and board in the park. Today a collection of his paintings hangs in the lobby of the Ahwahnee Hotel in Yosemite National Park. In 1934, Widforss was diagnosed with a serious heart ailment and was told to avoid high elevations like those at the Grand Canyon. On November 30, 1934, he suffered a heart attack while driving his car near El Tovar Hotel. This beloved Grand Canyon artist is buried in the pioneer cemetery, the final resting place of other early canyon residents, including Ralph Cameron, Pete Berry, and John Hance.

"AFTERNOON"—VIEW FROM THE WATCHTOWER, GRAND CANYON NATIONAL PARK, ARIZONA.   FROM PAINTING BY GUNNAR WIDFORSS.

Eight

GATEWAYS TO THE GRAND CANYON

Before arriving at the Grand Canyon, a traveler must pass through a town or small, seasonal tourist operation. These gateway communities offer food and a place to stay for the night. They also frame the park in all directions. Each gateway has a different perspective and creates a different point of reference for the visitor.

Williams, Arizona, was founded in 1880. This town is the official "Gateway to the Grand Canyon." Williams was originally a railroad supply and lumber town. The Santa Fe Railway put its spur line to the Grand Canyon from here in 1901 and built the Fred Harvey Company–run Fray Marcos Hotel in 1908. This town became the stopping-off point for most of the travelers to the Grand Canyon.

U.S. Highway 66 (Route 66) passes through Williams. Five mile east of town was the turnoff to the canyon, Highway 64. At the junction stood this road sign directing highway travelers either to Williams, in 5 miles, or to the Grand Canyon, in 57 miles. With the building of the interstate system, this sign became obsolete, and it has been removed.

Nearer the canyon, other small, seasonal tourist operations were in business. Since most of the tourists arrived in the summertime, these businesses were shuttered from fall until spring. Rowe's Well was located in the forest south of Hopi Point and had its own road up to the rim. Here accommodations included cabins with showers and wood-heated stoves, as well as a gas station. These buildings have been removed.

The Moqui Lodge stood at the south entrance of the park on Highway 64. A distinctive A-frame facade replaced an earlier clapboard building. This advertising postcard is for the beauty shop at Moqui Lodge that offered "that Miss America Look" for ladies vacationing at the Grand Canyon. The lodge stood on land leased from the forest service. When the lease was returned to the service, these buildings were removed.

Entering the park from the east, visitors would come through the Cameron Trading Post and Hotel. This business is situated where Highway 89 crosses the Little Colorado River. An early suspension bridge is located here. The elevation at Cameron is 4,195 feet. Very little precipitation falls at this location, making for an arid terrain. The banded hills of the Painted Desert are easily seen nearby.

The drive from the Cameron Trading Post and Hotel parallels the gorge created by the Little Colorado River and ascends to 7,400 feet at Desert View in the Grand Canyon. This roadway was once called the Navahopi Drive, since it lead to the Navaho and Hopi reservation lands. Here a 1930-postmarked card shows a viewpoint with the sheer 1,000-foot drop of the Little Colorado River gorge along the road.

From the north, visitors will come upon two small operations. The Jacob Lake Lodge was established in 1926–1927. The 8,770-foot elevation contrasts with that of the Cameron Trading Post and Hotel. Because of the great distances to drive to get to the North Rim, far fewer people are on the north side. The lodge is in the heart of the North Kaibab National Forest, the home of the Kaibab squirrel, which is found nowhere else.

The Kaibab Lodge is 5 miles from the north entrance of the Grand Canyon. The lodge was established in 1922 and was once part of the V. T. Ranch. Located in one of the meadows referred to as parks that are common on the North Rim, the lodge has food service, overnight accommodations, and a gas station. The surrounding parks have long been known for the viewing of wildlife.

THE GRAND CANYON. View in Havasu.

The west side of the Grand Canyon is the ancestral home the Havasupai people. These Native Americans reside in Cataract Canyon, a large side canyon of the Grand Canyon. Their village is along the Havasu Creek. Water from the creek is used for field crops and peach orchards that surround the village.

MOONEY FALLS, GRAND CANYON, ARIZ.

The waters of Havasu Creek dissolve the local limestone. This highly mineralized water reflects the color of the sky, turning the creek a turquoise blue. The creek cascades over a series of beautiful waterfalls. The four main falls are Supai, Havasu, Navajo, and Mooney. Travertine pools form at the base of these falls. This 1908-postmarked card shows the Mooney Falls.

BIBLIOGRAPHY

Anderson, Michael F. *Living at the Edge*. Grand Canyon, AZ: Grand Canyon Association, 1998.

Government Printing Office. *West Rim Drive in Grand Canyon National Park, Arizona*. Washington, D.C.: GPO, 1935.

Grattan, Virginia L., and Mary Colter. *Building upon the Red Earth*. Flagstaff, AZ: Northland Press, 1980.

Hinton, Wayne K., with Elizabeth A. Green. *With Picks, Shovels, and Hope*. Missoula, MT: Mountain Press Publishing Company, 2008.

James, George Wharton. *The Grand Canyon of Arizona*. Boston: Little, Brown and Company, 1910.

Kolb, Ellsworth L. *Through the Grand Canyon from Wyoming to Mexico*. New York: Macmillan Company, 1919.

Simpson, W. H. *El Tovar by Fred Harvey: A New Hotel at Grand Canyon of Arizona*. Chicago: Santa Fe Railway, 1905.

Tillotson, M. R. *Grand Canyon Country*. Stanford, CA: Stanford University Press, 1935.

Union Pacific Railroad. *Zion, Bryce Canyon, Grand Canyon National Parks*. Omaha, NE: W. S. Basinger Publisher, 1937.

Wright, Barton. *Hopi Material Culture*. Flagstaff, AZ: Northland Press, 1979.

www.arcadiapublishing.com

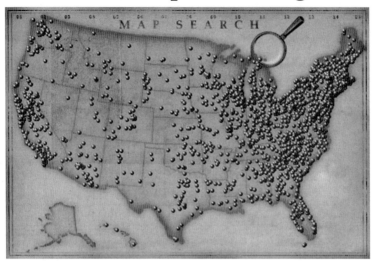

Discover books about the town where you grew up, the cities where your friends and families live, the town where your parents met, or even that retirement spot you've been dreaming about. Our Web site provides history lovers with exclusive deals, advanced notification about new titles, e-mail alerts of author events, and much more.

MADE IN THE USA

Arcadia Publishing, the leading local history publisher in the United States, is committed to making history accessible and meaningful through publishing books that celebrate and preserve the heritage of America's people and places. Consistent with our mission to preserve history on a local level, this book was printed in South Carolina on American-made paper and manufactured entirely in the United States.

This book carries the accredited Forest Stewardship Council (FSC) label and is printed on 100 percent FSC-certified paper. Products carrying the FSC label are independently certified to assure consumers that they come from forests that are managed to meet the social, economic, and ecological needs of present and future generations.

FSC

Mixed Sources
Product group from well-managed
forests and other controlled sources

Cert no. SW-COC-001530
www.fsc.org
© 1996 Forest Stewardship Council

Find Your Place in History.